Trying My Best

Katie Peters

GRL Consultants,
Diane Craig and Monica Marx,
Certified Literacy Specialists

Lerner Publications ◆ Minneapolis

Lerner Publications Company
An imprint of Lerner Publishing Group, Inc.
241 First Avenue North
Minneapolis, MN 55401 USA

For reading levels and more information, look up this title at www.lernerbooks.com.

Main body text set in Memphis Pro 24/39
Typeface provided by Linotype

Photo Acknowledgments
The images in this book are used with the permission of: © ArtBoyMB/Getty Images, pp. 12–13, 16 (left); © FatCamera/Getty Images, pp. 10–11, 16 (right); © guvendemir/Getty Images, pp. 14–15; © Jeff Greenough/Getty Images, pp. 4–5; © SDI Productions/Getty Images, pp. 8–9, 16 (center); © Shoji Fujita/Getty Images, pp. 6–7; © Sorapong Chaipanya/EyeEm/Getty Images, p. 3.

Front cover: © Fotokostic/Shutterstock Images.

Library of Congress Cataloging-in-Publication Data

Names: Peters, Katie, author.
Title: Trying my best / Katie Peters.
Description: Minneapolis : Lerner Publications, 2022. | Series: Be a good sport. Pull ahead readers. People smarts. Nonfiction | Includes index. | Audience: Ages 4–7 | Audience: Grades K–1 | Summary: "We don't have to be the best at every sport to have a good time. Trying our best will make the game way more fun! Pairs with the fiction title Dev Tries His Best"— Provided by publisher.
Identifiers: LCCN 2021010307 (print) | LCCN 2021010308 (ebook) | ISBN 9781728440958 (library binding) | ISBN 9781728444451 (ebook)
Subjects: LCSH: Sportsmanship—Juvenile literature.
Classification: LCC GV706.3 .P465 2022 (print) | LCC GV706.3 (ebook) | DDC 175—dc23

LC record available at https://lccn.loc.gov/2021010307
LC ebook record available at https://lccn.loc.gov/2021010308

Manufactured in the United States of America
1 – CG – 12/15/21

Table of Contents

Trying My Best

I try my best to throw.

I try my best to catch.

I try my best to kick.

I try my best to swim.

I try my best to skate.